Abortion
Recovery
For
Teens & Twenties

Heidi Heystek
Donna Steinke
©1998, first printing 1999
Revised 2012

This book is dedicated to our children,
victims of our abortion decisions
when we were teens.

Danielle

Inherent meaning ~ God is my judge
Spiritual connotation ~ Perceptive
Scripture ~ Psalm 119:112 NKJV
*"I have inclined by heart to perform your
statutes forever,
to the very end."*

Douglas

Inherent meaning ~ From the dark stream
Spiritual connotation ~ Adventurous
Scripture ~ I Corinthians 2:7 NKJV
*"But we speak wisdom of God in a hidden
mystery,
the hidden wisdom which God ordained
before the ages for our glory."*

We also dedicate this book to our families
who have been patient with us through the
healing process as well as in the process of
writing this book.

We thank Alternatives of Kalamazoo
Women's Care Center for their support of
our work and for their compassion for
the women and men who have been hurt by
abortion.

Welcome to *Abortion Recovery for Teens & Twenties.*
You have been through a difficult experience. We pray that God will use this book, combined with godly leadership, to bring healing to your soul, and to allow you to move forward with your life.

Contents

Group Rules

1. Confidentiality
2. Freedom to exit
3. Participation
4. Non-judgmental feedback
5. No rescuing
6. No interrupting
7. No monopolizing

Goal

To receive genuine and permanent healing from your post abortion emotional and spiritual pain, and to become the woman God created you to be.

"For I know the plans I have for you," declares the Lord, "plans to prosper you and not to harm you, plans to give you hope and a future."

Jeremiah 29:11

Chapter 1

Mind's Eye

Day 1

Read **Psalm 139:1-3**

1. According to verse 1, how well does God know you? _____

2. Fill in the blanks (from verse 2) "You know when I sit and when I _____: you perceive my _____ from afar."

3. This means that God knows your thoughts whether you feel close to him or not. Draw a heart on the line to show how close you feel to God right now. (Be honest!) ♥

_____
Very far away   not close or far   very close

4. Read Psalm 145:8-9. The goal of this Bible study is to take you down a path toward healing from your abortion experience. What does this verse tell you about God's concern for your pain?

_____

_____

*Finding peace with yourself
is a direct result
of finding
peace with God...*

Day 2

In this first chapter you will need to answer some tough questions. These questions will help you pinpoint specific areas about your abortion experience that you need to face. Please answer as completely and as honestly as possible.

Circle the best answer for each question.

1. Do you feel that there is a struggle going on inside of you? **yes   no**

2. Do you wrestle (emotionally) with your abortion decision or the people who took part in it? **yes   no**

3. Do you avoid passing by the places that remind you of your abortion, such as the clinic or hospital where the abortion was performed, or the drug store where your post-abortion prescription came from, etc.?

yes   no

4. Do you try to distract yourself with extra activities, work, or play, in order to avoid quiet times of self-reflection?   **yes   no**

5. Are you afraid to be alone?   **yes   no**

6. Do pictures that show a fetus bother you?
                                                yes   no

7. Do you feel anxious or angry when you see abortion clinic picketers, Life Chains, or any other pro-life demonstrations? **yes   no**

8. Are you uncomfortable being around pregnant women or people who have small children?   **yes   no**

9. Do you avoid the baby supply aisles in stores?   **yes   no**

10. Are you unable to sleep, or are you sleeping more than usual?   **yes   no**

11. Do you dream about being pregnant, or are you "haunted" by reoccurring nightmares of your aborted baby? **yes   no**

If yes, what is happening in these dreams?

_____
_____
_____
_____

_____

_____

_____

12. Are you moodier than you used to be? (Do you find yourself being bothered by even the smallest irritation? Do you snap at others, especially those close to you?)

yes   no

13. Are you and the baby's father still together?   **yes   no**

14. Have your relationships changed with your boyfriend, parents, family members, or friends since your abortion?   **yes   no**

If so, in what way have these relationships changed? _____

_____

_____

_____

15. Have either you or your boyfriend become abusive towards one another since the abortion? (Or have you recently entered into an abusive relationship?)

yes   no

16. Since your abortion, have you remained sexually active, or increased your sexual activity? **yes** **no**

17. Has your desire for a sexual relationship changed? **increased** **decreased** **same**

18. Have your eating habits changed? **yes** **no**

19. Do you find yourself eating more food in order to comfort yourself or to fill the "empty space"? **yes** **no**

20. Do you avoid eating to the point where you're becoming malnourished? **yes** **no**

21. Has your monthly period stopped due to weight loss? **yes** **no**

22. Have you gained or lost a significant amount of weight since your abortion? **yes** **no**

23. Are you currently using alcohol or drugs, perhaps as a way to numb the emotional pain from your abortion experience? **yes** **no**

24. If you have children, do you find that you are less attached to them than you'd like to be? **yes** **no**

11

25. Are you more protective of your children than is really necessary? **yes   no**

26. Have you put your focus on the future (your education, marriage, family, or career plans) in order to prove that your abortion was the best decision?   **yes·   no**

27. Do you have a strong desire to become pregnant again, perhaps to replace your aborted child?   **yes   no**

28. Do you think about escaping your current emotional pain by either running away or committing suicide? **yes   no**

29. If so, for how long have your felt this way? _____

30. Do you have a suicide plan? **yes   no**

31. Do you have flashbacks about the abortion procedure?   **yes   no**

32. Do you have panic attacks due to the flashbacks?   **yes   no**

33. Are you preoccupied with wondering if your baby was a boy or a girl, or what he or she would have looked like? **yes   no**

34. Are you drawn to children who are the

age your child would have been, or who look similar to how you imagine your child would have looked? **yes** **no**

35. Do you feel that you don't deserve to be loved or should be punished for having had an abortion? **yes** **no**

36. Do you believe that you have committed the "unpardonable sin" and that God could never forgive you for aborting your baby? **yes** **no**

37. Do you worry that God will eventually punish you or "even out the score" sometime in the future? **yes** **no**

38. Do you worry that you may never be able to have other children? **yes** **no**

39. Do you fear that if you have a child in the future that he or she will somehow be taken away from you, or will be born with birth defects and eventually die?

yes **no**

Count the number of questions you answered **yes** to. Record that number here _____.

If you have answered yes to ten or more questions, then this study will be of great benefit to you. If you answered **yes** to fewer than ten, but feel like you may still have unresolved problems related to an abortion, we encourage you to participate in the study as well. You do not need to be a Christian or interested in religion in order to benefit from this book either.

Many women who have had an abortion answer **yes** to many of these questions. The questions reflect issues that may come up for you before you are healed. Some women wait a long time before they begin to understand the ways their abortion(s) has (have) affected them. You will be better off if you decide now to continue this study. It's better to live in reality and face problems head on then to ignore them or wait until you're older to deal with them. Confronting these issues, even if it frightens you, will improve your relationships and will help you grow, especially in awareness of your value to God.

*Note- Although this book can be a self-study guide, the authors recommend working through the chapters with a leader in a small group or one on one setting. Don't hesitate to contact a counselor, pastor, the authors of this study, or a peer counselor at the local crisis pregnancy center in your area for further help.

Write a paragraph describing how you feel after answering the previous questions.

_____
_____
_____
_____
_____
_____
_____
_____
_____

What is your biggest concern about facing the choice you made to have an abortion?

_____
_____
_____
_____
_____

Day 3
Read **Psalm 147:3-6**

1. From verse 3, what kind of person does God help?

_____

2. Draw a picture that shows the condition of your heart right now.

God wants to heal your broken heart and bind up your wounds.

3. Look at verse four. What kind of person could count the stars and call them by name?

_____

_____

4. How big is God's ability to understand what we are thinking and feeling? _____

_____

_____

5. Summarize what you have learned about God from these verses? _____

_____

_____

_____

_____

_____

_____

Day 4

Read **John 10:1-10**

Jesus used stories to help people understand deep truths. In these verses He uses the example of a shepherd guarding his sheep.

1. How do the sheep respond to the shepherd's voice?

_____

2. The shepherd stands for the way Jesus wants to be in our lives. Picture Jesus as the shepherd and you as his sheep. In verse three you will find that the shepherd calls you by _____ and leads you out. He _____ ahead of you. (verse 4) You _____ him because you recognize his voice.

3. In verse eight, Jesus said, *"All who ever came before me were thieves and robbers."* Who do you feel has robbed you?

_____

4. Read verse nine. Jesus talks about the sheep finding pasture. What does a pasture do for a lamb? _____

Jesus wants you to be spiritually full to relieve your lifelong hunger.

5. Read verse ten. What is the goal of the thief? _____

And what is Jesus' goal?

_____

Day 5
Anniversary Syndrome

Many women who have had an abortion experience periods of depression around the date that their baby would have been due or around the date their abortion was performed. This is called **anniversary syndrome**. Write here the date of your abortion(s).

_____

_____

1. Looking back, do you recall a time when it was difficult just to make it through the day or week?   **yes   no**

2. Was it around either of the two anniversary dates?   **yes   no**

3. What are the ways in which you have coped with this so far?

_____

_____

_____

4. Did these behaviors help you or make things worse? _____
Why? _____

5. Look back over this week's lessons. What stands out to you as the most important part of the lesson?

_____

_____

_____

6. What is one thing you learned about God? _____

7. What is one thing you learned about yourself? _____

8. What part was hard for you to understand? _____

_____

_____

9. Do you think that you need this Bible study?   **yes   no**

10. Are you willing to do all of the lessons and come to group prepared to talk each time we meet?

If so, sign you name below.

_____   _____
Name   Date

NOTE: Please complete the abortion checklist located in the back of the book.

Talk to God

Pray this simple prayer. Add a few sentences of your own at the end. God loves you and wants you to know Him better.

Dear God, help me to understand the areas of my life where I need healing. Give me strength and courage to complete this Bible study, and begin to live my life the way you intend me to live. (Add your own words) Amen

Chapter Two

Daddy's Girl

"The absence of a mature father-child connection creates a void in the soul, a residual 'father-hunger'."
~ James Schaller, *The Search for Lost Fathering*

Day 1

Read Psalm 10:14, 17, 18

1. According to these verses, what does God see? _____

2. What does God do for the fatherless?

_____

3. Why does He do this? _____

_____

You find identity in a relationship with your father. Fathers set the model for what you might expect in relationships with men, even your future husband. A healthy, loving father protects, provides for and leads his family. Not all dads fall into this description.

Compare your father to God, who is called the heavenly father. If you were abused emotionally or physically, or if you were sexually violated by your dad or other significant men in your life, you may find it difficult to approach God as father. If you were abandoned or neglected by your father, you may fear that God will leave you too. Both of these issues deal with trust.

4. How would you describe trust? _____

_____

5. Give an example._____

_____

6. Put a check by the statements that best describe your dad:
___Warm and loving
___Physically present in your home, but not emotionally
___Neither physically, nor emotionally present
___A workaholic
___Demanding and controlling
___Physically and/or mentally abusive
___More nurturing than your mother
___Completely absent through death or abandonment
___Other:_____

Day 2

Even with a great dad, most people confuse the traits and character of God with their relationship with their earthly father. Because of this, God provided many stories, names, and examples of who He is, to help us sort out our distorted thinking. It is only through knowing God for who He truly is that we can have the best and fullest relationship with Him as possible.

Genesis 22:13-14 gives us an example of God as the Lord who will provide.

1. How did your father provide for your needs? _____

_____

_____

2. What role did your dad play in your abortion decision? _____

_____

_____

3. Some of your father's duties are listed. Put a star next to the ones that your dad did well. Underline an area of weakness for him.

To love and to bless, **Luke 15:20**
To teach, **Proverbs 1:8-9**

To guide and encourage, **I Thessalonians 2:11-12**

To command, **Deuteronomy 32:46**

To train and correct, **Ephesians 6:4**

To discipline, **Hebrews 12:4-8**

To supply need, **I Timothy 5:8**

4. Choose three of the verses listed above. Look them up in a Bible and write out the phrase that fits a father's job.

_____

_____

_____

_____

_____

_____

_____

"A FATHER TO THE FATHERLESS, A DEFENDER OF WIDOWS IS GOD IN HIS HOLY DWELLING." PSALM 68:5

Day 3

God the Father disciplines those He loves. When you hear the word discipline you may think of a spanking or a time out; but **discipline** means to train the mind or character of a person.

___Hebrew 12:5-8, ___Hebrews 12:10-11, ___Proverbs 12:1, ___Proverbs 13:18

1. Read at least three of the above sections of the Bible. Check off the ones your read. What did you learn? _____

_____

_____

2. Is discipline a good and loving thing?

                            yes   **no**

3. Why do we resist discipline?

_____

_____

_____

4. What is the cost of ignoring discipline?

_____

_____

_____

5. What is the reward of responding positively to discipline? _____

_____

_____

6. God expects you to honor and obey your parents.
Place a mark on the line below to show how well you obey and/or honor your parents.

_____

never obey   sometimes   usually   always obey

7. Read **Ephesians 6:1-3 and Proverbs 23:22-25.** What is your reward for honoring and obeying your parents? _____

_____

8. What are some ways you can honor your parents? _____

_____

_____

_____

_____

If you had a hard time coming up with anything, here are a few suggestions:

- Remember their birthday and anniversary
- Express appreciation for meals and help by cleaning up after dinner
- Don't criticize them to others

- Speak politely to them (please, thank you, excuse me, etc)
- Offer to help at home (bring in groceries, clean the house, cook a meal, wash the car)
- Bring your mom a bouquet of flowers for no special occasion

Day 4

Rebellion means to actively oppose authority. Maybe, because you struggle with trusting your parents, you have chosen to oppose them. You may resent something that they have done to you, or perhaps you are angry for what they did not do for you. God still expects you to submit to authority (unless you are being abused). He will honor your choice to obey them even though they aren't perfect. The following verses contain teaching about a rebellious attitude.

1. Read the verses and see how seriously God takes rebellion. Write the consequence on the line following the reference.
Proverbs 17:11

_____

Isaiah 30:1

_____

Ezekiel 20:38

I Samuel 15:23

Day 5

On the first day of this week, you were asked to define the word trust. Look back and see what you wrote. If you can trust someone, it is because they are faithful to you.

God, our father, is good and He is faithful. Even though bad things happen to us, He cares about us and walks through our pain with us. Even if your dad wasn't there for you when you were growing up, God will be.

"GOD IS OUR REFUGE AND STRENGTH, AN EVERPRESENT HELP IN TROUBLE." PSALM 46:1

Trust

You can trust someone if you're sure you can rely on their character, ability, strength, or truthfulness.

Faithfulness

You can believe someone is faithful if you trust him or her to stick with you and be loyal no matter what.

1. Read these verses and answer the questions.
Psalm 57:10 How far does God's faithfulness extend? _____

_____

Psalm 91:4-5 What is His faithfulness like?

_____

_____

_____

II Timothy 2:13 Does God's faithfulness depend on our behavior?   **yes   no**
Lamentations 3:19-23 What word is used to describe God's faithfulness? _____

2. Circle all the words that express how you felt during your abortion and the days that followed. They may seem contradictory but that's okay.

ALONE   PROTECTED   NEEDY
ABANDONED IGNORED GUILTY
SAD   RELIEVED   CARED FOR
LOVED   AFRAID   ANGRY

3. Do you believe that God cared about

what happened during your abortion procedure?   **yes**   **no**

4. God hears our cry. Which of these verses explains this the clearest to you?
Psalm 86:6-7 *"Hear my prayer, O Lord; listen to my cry for mercy. In the day of my trouble I will call to you for you will answer me."*
Psalm 34:17-18 *"The righteous cry out, and the Lord hears them; he delivers them from all their troubles. The Lord is close to the brokenhearted and saves those who are crushed in spirit."*

5. What impressed you about that verse?

_____
_____
_____
_____
_____

God wants every father to love his children like He does. God also wants every father to provide for and protect his children like He does. God expects fathers to be faithful and dependable, but many fathers just don't live up to God's standards.

If you find it difficult to open your heart to God, who is the perfect father, because you have a hard time separating His personality from your earthly dad who was not perfect, please pray the following prayer. Add a few sentences of your own at the end.

Talk to God

Dear God, as I am here talking to you I have to tell you that it is hard for me to believe that you are really different from my earthly dad.

*Please help me sort out in my mind the difference between the two of you. Help me to use the word **father** as you meant it to be used. I want to know you as a loving father.*

Help me to love my dad the way you do, with all his good and bad traits, and to learn to trust you more. (Add your own words)

Amen

Chapter 3

Mirror Image

Day 1

In the last chapter, you learned that a father's role is to give his children their identity, to protect, to provide for and to lead. The parent that tends to have the greatest influence in a child's life is the mother. She has the ability to set the "mood" of the home and is a constant molder of character.

1. How would you describe your mother?
___ Warm and loving
___Physically present, but not emotionally
___Neither physically, nor emotionally present
___A workaholic
___Demanding and controlling
___Physically and/or mentally abusive
___Completely absent through death or abandonment
___Your mother was the only "provider and leader"
___Other: _____

_____

Most mothers tend to be nurturing. They comfort us when we are sick or upset. God is a nurturer and comforter as well.

Here are some Bible verses that show some of the more motherly traits of God. He is usually thought of as our father in Heaven, but He has a very gentle, protective side as well.

"...how often I have longed to gather your children together, as a hen gathers her chicks under her wings..." **Luke 13:34**

"I will praise you, O Lord. Although you were angry with me, your anger has turned away, and you have comforted me."
Isaiah 12:1

"The Lord will surely comfort Zion and will look with compassion on all of her ruins."
Isaiah 51: 3

"I, even I, am He who comforts you..."
Isaiah 51:12-13

"As a mother comforts her child, so I will comfort you." **Isaiah 66:13**

"Blessed are those who mourn, for they will be comforted." **Matthew 5:4**

What promise did you find in these verses?

_____

33

Day 2

Femininity

"Your beauty should not come from outward adornment, such as braided hair and the wearing of gold jewelry and fine clothes. Instead, it should be that of your inner self, the unfading beauty of a gentle and quiet spirit, which is of great worth in God's sight."

I Peter 3:3-4

1. According to these verses, what makes a woman beautiful? _____

_____

_____

2. Why, do you suppose, inner beauty is more important to God than outer beauty?

_____

_____

3. Which is more important to many people in our culture: looking good or having a gentle spirit? (Think about magazines, commercials, popular music) What do you think about this? _____

_____

_____

_____

Mothers are our first and most lasting role model on femininity. Some may express their femininity by being submissive and passive. Others are more controlling and domineering. Many women have a hard time expressing any weakness or dependency on others. Some present themselves as needy and incapable of handling adult decisions.

4. Which of the above words fit your mom?

_____

5. Do you find yourself imitating her or trying to be the opposite? _____
Why? _____

_____

_____

The way your mother felt about men will also play a large role in the way you feel towards men.

6. How did/does your mother relate to your father, step-father, or her boyfriend? _____

_____

_____

7. Overall, do you think their relationship was/is **healthy** or **unhealthy**? (circle one)

8. Which words best describe their relationship? ___healthy ___lukewarm ___tolerant ___neglected ___emotionally abusive ___physically abusive
(We will cover more on relationships in Chapter 5)

9. According to God, several of a mother's duties are:
To be loving, **Exodus 2:1-4**
To protect, **II Kings 4:19-37**
To teach, **Proverbs 1:8-9**
To remember, **Luke 2:51**
To comfort, **Isaiah 66:11-13**
Choose one of the above sections of the Bible, look it up and write a summary of the verses._____

_____

_____

_____

_____

_____

_____

Day 3

Mother-Daughter Relationship
"The wise woman builds her house, but with her own hands the foolish one tears hers down." **Proverbs 14:1**

1. Give an example of a woman you know who has worked hard and with great wisdom to build a healthy environment for her children to grow up in.

Name _____ What she did:_____

_____

_____

What were the results?

_____

_____

2. Give an example of a mother whose choices and behavior led to the destruction of her family.

Name _____ What she did:_____

_____

_____

What were the results?

_____

_____

3. Some mothers are able to see beyond their own difficult circumstances in order to look out for their family's welfare. The story of Ruth and Naomi is an example of this. Although Naomi was Ruth's mother-in-law, Ruth loved her as if she were her own mother. Read the story in **Ruth 1:1-18.**

Describe how Ruth felt about Naomi.

_____

_____

Why do you think Ruth was so devoted to
Naomi? _____

_____

_____

How does your relationship with your own
mom compare? _____

_____

_____

4. When you were facing your decision to
abort your baby, did your mom know about
it? How did she react? _____

_____

_____

5. What were her fears regarding your
pregnancy? _____

_____

_____

6. What would you like to say to your
mother about your abortion experience?

_____

_____

_____

_____

_____

_____

_____

_____

Day 4

1. Which of the following examples best describes your mother's parenting? (circle the words)

Kinds of mothers:

Happy, **Psalm 113:9**   Noble, **Proverbs 31:29**   Reverence for God, **Proverbs 31:30** Prayerful- **Acts 12:12**   Troubled- **I Kings 17:17-24**   Cruel- **II Kings 11:1** Scheming- **I Kings 21:1-16**

2. Put a star next to two traits you would like to have as a woman. Look up those verses and write a brief summary here.

_____

_____

_____

_____

_____

3. Examples of Godly mothers:

Hannah_____**I Samuel 1**

Mary_____**Luke 1:26-56**

Elizabeth_____**Luke 1:5-13, 57-63**

Eunice and Lois_____**II Timothy 1:5**

Choose one of the women and read the verses that tell her story. Write next to her name what you respect about her.

Day 5

1. Have you had a hard time breaking away from your mother?   **yes**   **no**

2. Do you see her as lonely?

yes   **no**

3. Do you feel guilty for growing up?

yes   **no**

4. Have you ever felt that you needed to "cut the apron strings" because she never would be able to let go of you?

yes   **no**

5. Do you feel that she has given you love or attention that should have gone to a spouse (either because her husband wasn't around or because he wasn't emotionally available)?

yes   **no**

If you have checked yes for several of these, you need to question the emotional health of your relationship with your mom. There's a big difference between a natural love for a spouse and affection for our children.

Talk to God

If you feel the need to break this unhealthy bond, please pray these words:

Dear Heavenly Father, I want to pray for my mother. I ask that you would heal our relationship. Please help me respect her as the authority you have placed over me, but also show her that I am growing up. Help her to release me so that I can be free to become an adult. Also help her know that you will always be there for her even when I'm gone. (add your own words) In Jesus' name I pray, Amen.

6. Read through the following section of the Bible (The Message is a paraphrased translation). Circle all of the positive words you can find that describe this woman. Write here the number of words you circled._____

Proverbs 31:10-31 (The Message)

"A good woman is hard to find, and worth far more than diamonds. Her husband trusts her without reserve, and never has reason to regret it. Never spiteful, she treats him generously all her life long. She shops

41

around for the best yarns and cottons, and enjoys knitting and sewing. She is like a trading ship that sails to faraway places, she brings back exotic surprises. She's up before dawn preparing breakfast for her family and organizing her day. She looks over a field and buys it; then with the money she's put aside, plants a garden. First thing in the morning, she dresses for work, rolls up her sleeves, eager to get started. She senses the worth of her work, is in no hurry to call it quits for the day. She's skilled in the crafts of home and hearth, diligent in homemaking. She's quick to assist anyone in need, reaches out to help the poor. She doesn't worry about her family when it snows; their winter clothes are all mended and ready to wear. She makes her own clothing, and dresses in colorful linens and silks. Her husband is greatly respected when he deliberates with the city fathers. She designs gowns and sells them, brings the sweaters she knits to the dress shops. Her clothes are well-made and elegant, and she always faces tomorrow with a smile. When she speaks she has something to say, and she always says it kindly. She keeps an eye on everyone in her household, and keeps them busy and productive. Her children respect and bless her; her husband joins in with words of praise; "Many women have done wonderful things, but you've

*outclassed them all." Charm can mislead
and beauty soon fades. The woman to be
admired and praised is the woman who lives
in the Fear-of -God. Give her everything
she deserves. Festoon her life with
praises."*

7. Look back over this week's lessons.
What was the most important thing you
learned?

_____
_____
_____
_____
_____
_____

8. What kind of woman does God want you
to be? _____

_____
_____
_____
_____

9. What do you need to do to become that
kind of woman? _____

_____
_____
_____
_____

Chapter 4
The Pleaser

**"Faith never knows where it is
being led,
but it loves the One who is leading."**
~ Oswald Chambers

Day 1

The pleaser tends to be accommodating to others. This means that she works hard to fit in with others' expectations, needs, and desires, sometimes at great personal cost. This is a personality type often found in post-abortive women.

1. Do you feel like you have to be the strong or more mature person in close relationships?   **yes   no**

2. Do you feel that you have protected or even parented your mom and/or dad to some extent?   **yes   no**

3. Have you parented your brothers and sisters?   **yes   no**

4. If so, how do you feel about having that

responsibility? _____

_____

_____

5. If you resented it, have you rebelled as a result? **yes** **no**

6. Are you a perfectionist? **yes** **no**

7. Do you feel that you have such high expectations for yourself that you will never be able to live up to them? **yes** **no**

8. Have your parents placed their lost dreams on your shoulders? **yes** **no** If yes, give an example_____

_____

9. Do you feel that unless you're perfect your parents won't love or accept you for who you are?

yes **no**

10. No one is perfect. God tells us, *"As it is written: There is no one righteous, not even one; there is no one who understands, no one who seeks God"*, **Romans 3:10.** Put that verse in your own words, using your name to make it personal. _____

_____

_____

*"Our fathers have sinned and are no more,
and we bear their punishment."*
Lamentations 5:7

11. Do you feel that you carry the weight of
your family's failures or sins upon your
shoulders?   **yes**   **no**

12. Can you look back through your
family's history and see harmful habits or
patterns repeat again and again? Circle all
that apply:
adultery   alcohol or drug abuse
physical abuse   emotional abuse
sexual abuse   neglect
abandonment   divorce   abortion
pornography
other_____

These generational behaviors can create
family chains that tie us down and connect
us to the past. At times our own rebellion
secures the next link.

13. Would you like to break these chains?
Read **Isaiah 53:1-12.** These verses give a
brief summary of Jesus' purpose on earth.
According to these verses, what did it take
to break the cycle of sin and death?
_____
_____

_____

_____

_____

14. Read either **Luke 15:11-32** or **John 8:1-11.** Write a brief summary of the story in your own words. _____

_____

_____

_____

_____

15. What did you find in these verses that help you understand that you can be forgiven for the sin of abortion? How does that make you feel? _____

_____

_____

_____

_____

_____

_____

Day 2

The Way

A great thing about God is that He gives us second chances and new beginnings.

1. Choose two of the following verses. Look them up and find a group of words that indicates a new beginning.

Jeremiah 31:34_____
Matthew 26:28_____
Lamentations 3:22-23_____

God knew that we wouldn't be able to live up to all of his expectations and that our sin would separate us from him; so he made a way for us to come to him, by sending his son, Jesus, to be punished for all of our sins, so that we wouldn't have to be. This is essential if we are ever going to be as close to God as he wants to be with us.

"For the wages of sin is death, but the gift of God is eternal life in Christ Jesus the Lord."
Romans 6:23

When my husband and I dated we would always ask each other jokingly, how much do you love me? We would stretch out our arms wide and say, this much! Years later on the day we joined the church and dedicated our children to the Lord, a friend remembering this, gave us a picture for a gift. It read, I asked Jesus how much do you love me? This much, he answered, then He stretched out His arms and died.
~Heidi Heystek

Jesus' perfect and sinless life was the only way to build a bridge between us and the heavenly Father so we can have a relationship with Him. As His body hung on the cross, stretched out between heaven and earth, he prayed for us, asking "Father forgive them, for they do not know what they are doing." God placed all of our sins on Jesus. He is our salvation and our only way to escape what we deserve.

2. Read the following verses. Why is Jesus the only one qualified to save us?

_____

_____

Jesus is the perfect mediator between God and man. **Hebrews 3:1-6, 4:14-16**
He is the Holy One of Israel, the only one who is morally perfect. **Isaiah 1:4**
Jesus did not come to call the righteous, but the unrighteous. **Mark 2:17, Psalm 143:2**
The Lord became our righteousness... **Psalm 143:1**
...for we knew no righteousness. **Romans 3:10**
Christ died for sinners. **Romans 5:6-11, Hebrews 9:27-28**

"Therefore confess your sins to each other, and pray for each other so that you may be

49

healed." **James 5:16**

"If we confess our sins, He is faithful and just and will forgive our sins and purify us from all unrighteousness." **I John 1:9**

"But when the kindness and love of God our Savior appeared, he saved us, not because of righteous things we have done, but because of his mercy. He saved us through the washing of rebirth and renewal by the Holy Spirit, whom he poured out on us generously through Jesus Christ our Savior, so that, having been justified by his grace, we might become heirs having the hope of eternal life. **Titus 3:4-7**

3. The word righteous means goodness, acting in a just and upright way. As you reread the preceding verses circle the words that express the idea of righteousness.

4. Is it because of your own goodness that you can come to God?   **yes   no**

5. What does it take to come to God?

_____
_____
_____
_____
_____

Day 3

The Enemy

In your daily decisions, you struggle between choosing to do what is good and making sinful choices. God is on your side. He is always pulling for you to do what is good. Satan wants to see you fail and be destroyed.

In the Bible you can find many verses that tell you about the evil, destructive nature of Satan, or the Devil. He was once called Lucifer, who was an angel. When he chose to rebel he was cast out of heaven.

"The devil prowls around as a roaring lion seeking whom he may devour." **I Peter 5:8**

Hell is a place of eternal torment which was prepared for the devil and his angels.

Matthew 25:41; Revelation 19:19-20

Through Jesus' death and resurrection, Jesus now holds the keys to death and hell.

Revelation 1:17-18

1. Look up the verses that follow, then fill in the blanks using the following words to describe Satan.

Enemy, captive, lies, spiritual force of evil, roaring lion, murderer, god of this age, accuser, and serpent.

Satan is our _____ in **Revelation 12:10**
He is our _____ in
I Peter 5:8 and is like a _____.
The father of all _____ and a
_____ in **John 8:44**
The _____ in **II Corinthians 4:4**
The _____ in **Ephesians 6:12**
The _____ in **Genesis 3:1**
Satan takes us _____ to do his will
in **II Timothy 2:26**

Day 4

Temptation

Do you sometimes find yourself wanting to do things that you know are wrong and are bad for you? This is called temptation; a spiritual battle of right and wrong going on inside of you.

Paul wrote in **Romans 7:15-20** about this. Verse 19 says, *"For what I do is not the good I want to do; no, the evil I do not want to do-this I keep on doing."*

"Since the children have flesh and blood, he too shared in their humanity so that by his

death he might destroy him who holds the power of death, that is, the devil, and free those who all their lives are held in slavery by their fear of death." **Hebrews 2:14-15**

"Because he himself suffered when he was tempted, he is able to help those how are being tempted." **Hebrews 2:18**

"I am the way and the truth and the life. No one comes to the Father except through me." **John 14:6**

"For it is by grace you have been saved through faith, and this not from yourselves, it is the gift of God, not by works, so that no one can boast." **Ephesians 2:8-9**

1. Which words in the above verses describe what salvation is? (for example: way)

_____

_____

_____

2. Read the following definitions of repentance and penance.

Penance-an act of self-humiliation, self-inflicted pain, or devotion performed to show sorrow for sin.

Repentance-to turn away from sin and dedicate yourself to making your life right.

Explain in your own words the difference between penance and repentance._____

_____
_____
_____
_____

Which one do you believe God expects from you? Why? _____

_____
_____
_____
_____

Talk to God

Would you like to enter into a personal relationship with God? If so, please pray this simple prayer:

Dear Jesus, I have sinned against you. But I now understand that you came and died in my place. I open my heart and mind to you and receive you as my personal Lord and Savior. Thank you for forgiving my sins and setting me free. Please come into my heart and my life, and make me the person you have always intended me to be. Fill me with your spirit. I ask this in your precious name, Amen!

The Bible tells us that the angels rejoice in heaven when a soul is saved. If you prayed for salvation, the angels are throwing a party in your honor right this minute! **Luke 15:10**

Below are three chapters from the Bible which may help you express your feelings at this moment. Choose at least one of the chapters and read it aloud. **Psalm 25, Psalm 103, Psalm 138**

3. Could you relate to the feelings expressed by the writer of the chapter you choose?   **yes   no**

4. If yes, how were his feelings similar to your own? _____

_____

_____

_____

_____

Day 5

1. Look up **Isaiah 12:2.** Fill in the blanks, "Surely God is my _____; I will trust and not be _____. The Lord, the Lord, is my _____ and my _____; he has become my salvation."

2. Jesus died to become our Savior. He took the punishment for our sin. He died so we can live in heaven with him forever. What motivated God to send his son Jesus to earth to pay for your sin? **John 3:16**

Through Jesus and his sacrifice we are now able to come to the throne of God. Look in the following verses to find out what that means and why we want to come into God's presence.

Hebrews 4:16, 10:19-22 What do you receive at the throne of grace? _____

Ephesians 2:18, 3:12 How may we approach God? _____

John 14:6 What is the only way to come to the Father? _____

You are now a child of God, a new creation! *"Therefore, if anyone is in Christ, he is a new creation; the old has gone, the new has come."* **II Corinthians 5:17**

You have been adopted into God's family as his daughter and are now his heir. *"...to redeem those under the law, that we might receive the full rights of sons. Because you are sons, God sent the Spirit of his Son into*

56

our hearts, the Spirit who calls out, 'Abba, Father!' So you are no longer a slave, but a son; and since you are a son, God has made you also an heir."
Galatians 4:5-7

3. What are some of the differences between a slave and a son? _____

_____

_____

_____

4. How is this change in relationship significant to you? _____

_____

_____

_____

The Gift of the Holy Spirit

As our loving Father, God gives us the Holy Spirit to help us in our everyday life. *"In the same way, the Spirit helps us in our weakness. We do not know what we ought to pray for, but the Spirit himself intercedes for us with groans that words cannot express."*
Romans 8:26

5. According to this verse, what does the Holy Spirit do for us? _____

_____

6. Why is this important?

_____

_____

7. Read **Luke 11:9-13.** The Holy Spirit is compared to a good _____.

"I pray that out of his glorious riches he may strengthen you with power through his Spirit in your inner being, so that Christ may dwell in your hearts through faith. And I pray that you, being rooted and established in love, may have power, together with all saints, to grasp how wide and long and high and deep is the love of Christ, and to know this love that surpasses knowledge-that you may be filled to the measure of all the fullness of God."
Ephesians 3:16-19

8. Circle the benefits God offers you listed in the above verses. (example: strengthen)

Memorize the above three verses from Ephesians, and quote them to your group leader. When you struggle with feeling unworthy of love, quote these verses to yourself.

Chapter 5
Looking for Love
Day 1

1. Everyone wants to be loved and to love. Have you ever felt really loved and cared for?   **yes   no**

2. Sometimes we look for love in the wrong places, and for the wrong reasons. We get hooked on romance and miss out on real love. The difference between romance and true love is explained below.

Romance- Romance is a quick but short-lived fix for loneliness. It is a feeling that is pleasurable, and is a "mutually shared dreamy version of oneself and one's partner".
 ~ Jim Tally and Bobbie Reed, *Too Close Too Soon*

True Love- Love is defined in **I Corinthians 13.** Look it up and write a definition for true love. _____

_____

_____

_____

_____

3. How would you describe your relationship with the father of your baby before the abortion?

Close   distant   just met   just friends

4. How would you describe your relationship following you abortion?

Close   distant   non-existent   still friends

5. If your relationship has changed considerably, how would you explain what happened?

_____

_____

_____

_____

Sex outside of marriage

Many young men and women whose parents haven't taught them from the Bible have no idea what standards God has set up for sexuality. Some may believe that God doesn't care. Others may believe that He is opposed to sex. The truth is He cares very much. He created physical intimacy as a gift to be enjoyed within the safety of a committed marriage relationship.

6. Choose at least three out of the five following sections of the Bible to read, and then write out what you learned.

II Timothy 2:22_____
I Corinthians 6:18_____
I Corinthians 5:9-11_____
I Corinthians 6:9_____
Ezekiel 16:3-16_____

Day 2

1. The following verse from **I Thessalonians 4:3-8** provide a clear picture of what God wants from us. Underline the specific commands.

"It is God's will that you should be sanctified: that you should avoid sexual immorality; that each of you should learn to control his own body in a way that is holy and honorable, not in passionate lust like the heathen, who do not know God; and that in this matter no one should wrong his brother or take advantage of him. The Lord will punish men for all such sins, as we have already warned you. For God did not call us to be impure, but to live a holy life. Therefore, he who rejects this instruction does not reject man but God, who gives you his Holy Spirit."

God created sex for a very special relationship called marriage **(I Corinthians 7:2)**. He planned sex as a part of an intimate marriage relationship to protect us physically, spiritually and emotionally, not

61

to prevent us from experiencing pleasure. Because of His love and concern for us, He gives us these very specific guidelines.

Sin for a season

2. What is the difference between **love** and **lust?** Look in these verses, and then contrast the two words. **I John 4:7-21, I John 2:16-17, James 1:13-15, Proverbs 7**

LOVE   LUST

3. In **Colossians 3:5** God says, *"Put to death, therefore, whatever belongs to your earthly nature: sexual immorality, impurity, lust, evil desires and greed, which is idolatry."* What are several ways you can put to death lust and impurity? _____

_____

_____

If you need some suggestions, look up **Galatians 5:16-25.**

Day 3

True Love
Agape love is Godly love that is given without condition and is not deserved.

(Romans 5:8) *"Dear friends, let us love one another, for love comes from God."* **I John 4:7-12**

"Love is patient, love is kind. It does not envy, it does not boast, it is not proud. It is not rude, it is not self-seeking, it is not easily angered, it keeps no record of wrongs. Love does not delight in evil but rejoices with the truth. It always protects, always trusts, always hopes, and always perseveres. Love never fails." **I Corinthians 13:4-8a**

1. What is the hardest part of loving someone in this way? Why?_____

_____
_____
_____
_____
_____
_____

Day 4

Second Virginity

God loves and forgives us. You can start over! Begin by committing to staying pure and entering marriage knowing you can resist temptation with the help of God.

1. Read **I Peter 2:11.** Is it easy to turn away from the old ways of behaving?

yes no

What do these verses compare the struggle to? _____

2. *"For the grace of God that brings salvation has appeared to all men. It teaches us to say 'no' to ungodliness and worldly passions, and to live self-controlled, upright and godly lives in this present age...* **Titus 2:11-12**

From the message in these two verses, do you think it is possible to live self-controlled and godly lives? **yes no**

Why or why not? _____

_____

Breaking soul ties

Soul ties are intimate connections we have made with other people. In order to have a healthy marriage relationship, we must give up all former ties, emotional, physical and spiritual.

Intimacy is like two pieces of paper glued together. No matter how quickly you try to pull them apart, some of each paper sticks to the other. **We need to ask God's help in releasing us from unhealthy relationships.**

3. Make a list of anyone you need to cut soul ties with. Then pray the prayer below or ask with your own words for help from your heavenly Father.

_____

_____

_____

_____

Talk to God

Dear Heavenly Father, I ask you now to help me release unhealthy connections that I have with other people that are not pleasing to you. I know I can't do this on my own. I need your strength and power to cut the emotional, physical, and spiritual ties I have formed with my past relationships.

Please take from my memory (name those you listed above). Make this cut complete, so that in the future I won't compare my husband to the men/relationships from my past. I want to start over, allowing for my future relationships to be pure, even in my thoughts. Thank you, Father, for your concern for these details in my life and for your mighty power to deliver me from it all. Amen.

4. How did talking to God about this make you feel? _____

_____

_____

5. What will you do if you feel tempted to
fantasize about past soul ties? _____

_____

_____

_____

Day 5

Choosing a Husband

When it comes to selecting a husband,
choose carefully.   If you were lonely
growing up, or lacking a father's love, be
especially   cautious-you   are   particularly
vulnerable when it comes to relationships
with the opposite sex. Ask for counsel from
people who care about you and your future
well-being.

Make sure that you choose a man who
demonstrates   maturity   and   commitment.
Marriage is for adults; it is not a game.
Love should be shared from the overflow of
your heart-not manipulated from another
person in order to fill up your empty heart.

Mature people think, act, and then feel, in
that order.   Immature people feel, act and

then think about it later. Many cultures demand instant everything, from instant photos and instant food, to instant relationships and instant divorces. This trend has created a weakened society and caused many hearts to be broken.

1. Leviticus 18 describes who to avoid as a marriage partner. Read the chapter, and write what you learned. _____

_____

_____

_____

_____

_____

Ask God in daily prayer to lead you to a mate who will be a godly leader. Pray that God would prepare his heart, to love you as Christ loved the church and to never hold your past against you. Ask God to prepare you to be a loving wife who can demonstrate grace and experience soul satisfying intimacy with your husband. Ask God to teach you self-control so from this point on you will keep yourself pure for this lifetime mate.

2. Read **I Corinthians 7:1-11.** How can these marriage guidelines be a safeguard for you?_____

_____

_____
_____
_____

3. Look up either **I Peter 3:1-7** or
Ephesians 5:22-33. These verses explain
the role of husband and wife.
What is the role of the husband? _____

_____
_____

What is the role of the wife? _____

_____
_____

4. How would these roles, designed by God,
be helpful in a marriage relationship?

_____
_____
_____
_____

5. In what way might they seem difficult to
follow? _____

_____
_____

6. *"Let marriage be held in honor among
all, and let the marriage bed be undefiled;
for fornicators and adulterers God will
judge."* **Hebrews 13:4**

According to this verse, is God serious about our purity and our faithfulness to our spouse in marriage?   **yes**   **no**

7. What is the most important lesson you learned this week? _____

_____
_____
_____
_____
_____
_____

Talk to God

Dear Heavenly Father, I know that you want only the best for me in every part of my life. I ask that you will prepare the spouse you have chosen for me. Bring a man into my life who loves you and who won't judge me, but will overlook my past.

Lord, I ask that you cleanse me from within so I will be able to present myself as a pure bride to my future husband. Give me the strength to remain pure in my intimate life, to save my sexuality from now on for my future husband, so my wedding night can truly be the time of passion you intend it to be. (add your own words) Amen.

Chapter 6

Mommy

Day 1

This week we will turn our focus on the baby that was lost as a result of the abortion procedure and your reaction to losing him or her. Whether you have thought about it yet or not, you are a parent, whether your baby is here on earth or up in heaven. (We refer in this book to baby in the singular, but if you have had multiple babies and/or abortions, you will be thinking about each one of them.)

1. How do the following verses describe the child before birth? **Ecclesiastes 11:5, Psalm 139:13-16, Luke 1:41-44**_____

_____

_____

_____

_____

2. Look up **Jeremiah 1:5.** Where was the child first conceived? _____

_____

_____

The Stages of Grief

When you lose someone because of death, you can expect to react in ways that are common to most people. You may not follow the same order as another person's grieving, and you may feel like you are bouncing around among the various stages. But understanding the concepts of the stages of grief will help you as you realize that you have truly lost someone significant to you - your own little baby.

The stages are as follows: relief, denial, bargaining, and acceptance.

Relief is one of the first stages in the grief process. It is usually short-lived when it comes to responding to an abortion. As a result, denial may quickly take its place.

Denial is to be dishonest with yourself, or self-deception. It may last several weeks, months, or even years, depending upon your ability and willingness to cope with your strong feelings about the abortion.

To deny something or someone is to declare it untrue. With abortion, you may do this in the effort to disconnect emotionally from your unborn child in order to avoid having to deal with your painful emotions associated with this type of loss.

Luke 22:34, 54-62 speaks about Peter and his denial of Christ. Notice that Jesus, back in **Luke 22:31, 32** already knew that Peter would deny him. Just as the crowing rooster broke Peter's denial, something will usually trigger our locked up emotions in order for God to begin to break through our denial.

3. What are some of the ways that you sense God has begun to help you break through the denial in your life?

_____

_____

_____

_____

_____

A break in denial usually leads into the stage of **bargaining.**

Bargaining means to negotiate or to make acceptable. You may think that you can make up for the abortion by doing good things for others or by having another baby and being the best mom you can be. Yet, sooner or later you will come to the point where you know that nothing can make your abortion, nor the situation that led up to it, acceptable. When you reach the end of yourself, you are in the place where you will be met by God and His grace. Then you can finally come to the point of **acceptance.**

72

The stage of **acceptance** allows you to accept the fact that the abortion ended your unborn child's life. The next step will be to understand and accept that this sin is now covered under the blood of Jesus and God does not hold it against you any longer.

Day 2
Created in God's Image

An **image** is a sculpted likeness: a duplicate, or other reproduction of an object. It is something that closely resembles another.

1. In whose image were you created? See **Genesis 1:27** and **Genesis 2:7.** _____

_____

_____

Historical Roots

Some post-abortive women struggle with the need to isolate themselves from others. If you are dealing with this, remember you are not the only one who has ever aborted a baby. Abortion has been around since there were unwanted pregnancies. Satan will try to isolate you in order to attack you. **Psalm 106:37-38**

2. In Leviticus, the Bible records the story of the Ammonites who sacrificed their children to Molech, one of their many gods. Read **Leviticus 18:21** and **20:3.** Why did they sacrifice their children? _____

_____

_____

3. King Ahab and his wife Jezebel worshipped Baal and Asherah which believed in the sacrificing of children. Read about it in **I Kings 16:30-33.** What does God say about this in **Jeremiah 32:35?**

_____

_____

_____

4. Matthew 9:13 says, *"I (God) desire mercy, not sacrifice."* How does this relate to the Old Testament verses?

_____

_____

_____

5. Reflect upon your personal role in the abortion. You had both internal and external pressures. Internal pressures are your own fears, dreams, hopes, needs. List some of those here. _____

_____

_____

_____
_____
_____
_____

External pressures are circumstances and
people that influenced your decision. List
some of those here.

_____
_____
_____
_____
_____
_____
_____

6. How was your abortion like a child
sacrifice?

_____
_____
_____
_____

How was it
different?_____
_____
_____
_____
_____

Day 3

Who Controls the Womb?

Many modern teachings, particularly in sex education classes, could have led you to believe that a woman can completely control when or if she becomes pregnant. These philosophies don't account for God's plan or timing. In **Psalm 127:3,** the Bible clearly tells us that children are a gift from God.

1. Fill in the following blanks.

He will _____the fruit of your womb. **Deuteronomy 7:13**

He _____ the womb.
Genesis 20:18

He _____ the womb.
Genesis 29:31 & 30:22

He causes the womb to
_____**Luke 1:31**

2. God gives us the ability to bear children. Were you aware of this truth prior to your abortion?   **yes   no**

3. Would it have made a difference in your decision to abort?   **yes   no**

Talk to God

After thinking through the loss of your child, you may begin the natural process of grieving. If you are saddened over this, please pray these words.

Dear Lord, You already know that I have sinned by taking the life of my child. I ask you to forgive me for being disobedient and selfish. You are the only one who truly knows the motives I had for taking that precious life you gave me, and you alone can grant me peace and forgiveness. Help me to accept your gift of forgiveness and to live at peace with You as the center of my life. Amen.

4. On a separate piece of paper, write a letter to your aborted child. Tell him or her everything you have wanted to say, but never had the chance.

5. What do you imagine your child would want to say to you right now, in response to your letter? _____

_____

_____

_____

_____

_____

_____

_____

6. Read the story of David and Bathsheba. **II Samuel 11-12: 1-23.** Based on these verses, where do you think your baby is now?

_____

7. Have you come to a point of believing that the child that you lost through the abortion was your own flesh and blood, a unique individual who is precious to God?

yes   no

Look up **Psalm 139:13-16** and **Jeremiah 1:5** for further confirmation.

8. For many women, a part of healing from an abortion is to name their aborted child. Ask God to help you choose a name that means something special and one that will reflect the value of this child as a dignified member of your family. This helps you to identify him or her as a reality in your life and will give the baby a place in your past, your present, and your future. The event and the memory are always going to be there for you, but now they will have a place. Write gender and name(s) here:

_____

* When you are ready, please share the name(s) with your peer counselor or pastor. They will be used during a very special memorial service that will be held in your baby's honor at the completion of this study.

Day 4

Mourning

Mourning is a necessary and normal expression in times of great sorrow. The Bible does not say, *if* we mourn, it says *when* we mourn. **Matthew 5:4, Isaiah 61:2**

In the days when the Bible was written, people who were mourning responded in ways that may seem foreign to us, but were normal then. They would tear their clothes **(Esther 4:1-3, II Samuel 3:31-32),** neglect their appearance, (**II Samuel 19:24),** and some people would wear old rags and cover their faces with ashes, **(Genesis 37:34).**

In current cultures, people mourn in other ways: crying, not eating, wearing specific colored clothing, wanting to be alone, wanting to talk constantly about what has caused their grief, or not wanting to talk about it at all.

1. Have you personally expressed your sorrow in any of these ways?_____ If yes, circle the ways. Write any other ways here:

_____

Idols

If you had your abortion to "protect" someone else, Satan has used your natural nurturing instinct against you. You were pulled between which to nurture: the people on the outside of your womb, or the one on the inside. By concerning yourself with the welfare of other people in this matter, you chose to place their needs above God's plan and created an idol. An idol is anything or anyone you place above God.

2. Look up the commandment that teaches about idols and summarize what it says. **Exodus 20:4** _____

_____

_____

3. Read **I Corinthians 10:13-14.** What are you supposed to do when you are tempted to make something or someone else an idol?

_____

4. Who or what was your idol during the time that you decided to have an abortion?

_____

_____

Talk to God

If you would like to break free from your idols, please pray these words.

Father God, I have put others before you, letting them become idols in my life and giving them what should have been saved for you. Forgive me for not putting you first, and help me to do that from this point on. Help my thoughts and actions honor you and reflect what is important to you. Give me strength to resist the idols around me so that I will worship only you. Amen.

Day 5
Others Who Took Part

1. Did your parents or guardians force you to have an abortion?   **yes**   **no**

If you circled yes, what were their reasons?

_____
_____
_____

2. If your parents or guardians do not know about the abortion, do you plan on telling them sometime in the future?

yes   **no**

If you circled no, what would stop you?

_____

_____

_____

3. Is there anyone else you have hidden
your abortion form? If so, why? _____

_____

_____

_____

_____

4. Do you plan to tell them some day? If
yes, how would you begin to tell them this
information?

_____

_____

_____

_____

5. Are you afraid that they would reject you
if they knew?   **yes**   **no**

When and if you do become a mother again,
love your children with all of your heart, but
always understand that they belong to God
and that they are only yours for a short time.
They will eventually grow up and move
away. You'll have to be careful, especially
as a post-abortive woman, not to make your
children your entire life. Mothers who do

this have a hard time letting their children become independent. Remember to work for a healthy balance between motherhood and who you are as a person apart from your children.

Forgiveness

Following your abortion, the enemy will often try to torment you with flashbacks or nightmares pertaining to your abortion experience or the child that was lost as a result. If you have already prayed for forgiveness, you are approved of by God because you are in Christ Jesus and his atonement covers the past. If you are still feeling tormented, please pray these words:

Talking to God

Dear Heavenly Father, I ask that my nightmares and flashbacks be stopped in the name of Jesus. I ask that you would renew my mind through the power of your Holy Spirit. I have asked for your forgiveness and have received it. Jesus has paid my debt in full. I know this and trust in the power of his mighty name to keep me. Amen.

"You turned my wailing into dancing; you

removed my sackcloth and clothed me with joy, that my heart may sing to you and not be silent. O Lord my God, I will give you thanks forever." **Psalm 30:11-12**

Chapter 7
A Matter of Choice
Day 1

Anger

God commands us to get rid of anger
(James 1:19-21).
Anger hurts you more if you hold on to it
than it hurts the person who you are angry
with. You may think that if you let go of the
anger then you will be letting the other
person "off the hook", and then they won't
experience consequences for hurting you.
This simply isn't true.

God's anger is different from ours. He is
slow to become angry **(Nehemiah 9:17).**
He would rather show us mercy.

1. Are you still feeling angry at anyone who
was a part of your abortion experience? List
those people, including yourself if it applies.

_____

_____

_____

_____

_____

Attitude

You can't control other people's actions or feelings, but one area you can learn to control is your attitude. You can choose whether or not to let someone affect your life with his or her opinions. Just because someone has a negative opinion of you does not mean that you have to own his or her perceptions.

Paul writes in **Titus 3:3,** *"At one time we too were foolish, disobedient, deceived and enslaved by all kinds of passions and pleasures. We lived in malice and envy, being hated and hating one another."*

In verse nine he wrote: *"avoid foolish controversies and genealogies and arguments and quarrels about the law, because these are unprofitable and useless."* Verses 10-11 teach...*"warn a divisive person once, and then warn him a second time. After that, have nothing to do with him. You may be sure that such a man is warped and sinful; he is self-condemned."*

2. Go back through the previous verses, and circle any sins that you have been involved in.

3. List here the sin that you think has been the most damaging in your relationships.

_____
_____
_____
_____
_____
_____

Day 2

"He who covers an offense promotes love, but whoever repeats the matter separates close friends." **Proverbs 17:9**

Forgiving Others

It's impossible to get through life without being hurt by others. When you have been hurt it is natural to hold on to it and to feel angry. God wants and expects you to respond differently however.

1. What do the following verses tell you about forgiving others? Choose 3 of the 5

Matthew 6:12 _____
Matthew 18:21-22 _____
Mark 11:25 _____

Ephesians 4:32 _____
I Peter 3:8-12 _____

2. Can you trust God and His justice enough
to let go of hurt and anger toward those who
have hurt you?   **yes   no**

3. Read **Psalm 56:1-6.** David is praying to
God about the way his enemies pursue him
and attack him.   What conclusion does
David come to? _____

_____

_____

4. Forgiving others requires that you choose
to let go of your right to remain angry.
Remember it is a choice, not a feeling.
Holding on to your anger almost always
leads to bitterness. Read **Ephesians 4:31.**
What does God want you to do with any
bitter feelings? _____

_____

_____

5. Bitterness comes from thinking over and
over about the way someone has hurt you.
If you don't deal with bitterness, it grows
like a prickly weed and hurts you more in
the end more than it does the other person.
In addition to your ongoing hurt and anger,
it gives Satan permission to remain active in
your life. Look up 3 of the following verses

and write a paragraph describing what you have learned. **Matthew 6:14-15, Proverbs 20:22, Hebrews 12:15, I Corinthians 13:4-7, 11; Galatians 5:22**

_____

_____

_____

_____

_____

_____

_____

_____

_____

_____

_____

Day 3

Getting Even

"Never take your own revenge, beloved, but leave room for the wrath of God, for it is written, Vengeance is mine, I will repay, says the Lord." **Romans 12:19 (NAS)**

God will judge the wrong behavior of others; you don't need to do it for him. **I Corinthians 4:5, II Peter 2:4-10**

God, who has forgiven us, expects us to forgive others in return. In doing so, you are not only released from your offenders, but you are released from those you have offended. Read **Matthew 18:23-35.** What happened to the unforgiving servant?

_____

_____

Love your enemies, and pray for them.
Matthew 5:44

You will reap what you sow, so make sure you are sowing things of God.
Luke 6:37-38, Galatians 6:7-8

1. Who is someone who has wronged you? Put his or her initials here._____

2. From the above verses, what is God asking you to do about this person? _____

_____

_____

_____

_____

Anger tends to run side by side with fear a lot of the time. You may express your deep fears in an angry way because you feel strong showing anger and vulnerable when you show your fear.

Fear

3. Read **I John 4:18, Romans 8:15,** and **Isaiah 51:12.** What verse impressed you the most, and what did you learn from it? _____

_____

_____

_____

_____

_____

The Lord is Peace

God wants to give you peace that is out of the ordinary; it goes beyond your ability to understand.

4. If you are willing to forgive others, God will quiet your inner storm. He will become your peace, because He is the only one who is able to give the kind of peace that passes all understanding. **Philippians 4:4-9, Judges 6:24**

When you trust in the Lord and have his peace, you no longer need to worry. As life goes on, you'll realize that God works for the good of those who love him, even when you're going through deep sorrow and it seems that this cannot be true. *"If God is for us who can be against us?"* **Romans 8:31b**

5. What are some things that worry you?

_____

_____

_____

You can ask the Lord to carry your worries for you. Choose one of these verses, and write it below. **Matthew 6:25-27, Mark 4:19, Luke 8:14**

_____

_____

_____

_____

_____

_____

Peace in Relationships

"Make every effort to live in peace with all men and to be holy; without holiness no one will see the Lord." **Hebrews 12:14**

When you become hurt or offended in the future, learn to offer to others the grace that God has given to you. At times you may have to remind yourself that you already forgave a particular person who has hurt you. That person may not feel in need of

92

your forgiveness, because he or she may not understand the pain you have endured. However, in forgiving you will have done your part, and God will honor you for that. Remember: if you hold on to your anger, it will get in the way of your prayers. You need to choose whether or not the offense is worth coming between you and the Lord. Read **Psalm 66:18**

6. What is God telling you to do to pursue peace in your relationships right now?

_____

_____

_____

_____

_____

_____

7. Will you obey Him? _____

8. Memorize **Hebrews 12:14,** recite it to your group leader the next time you meet.

Day 4
When Disagreements Come

Speak the truth in love.
1. Read the following verses. How could you avoid or end a disagreement based on the teaching in the verses? **Ephesians 4:15;**

Romans 12:14, 19-21; Proverbs 15:16

_____
_____
_____
_____
_____
_____

2. You cannot always please people and God at the same time. **(Luke 6:26)** Sometimes you have to choose between the two. **(Matthew 6:24)** _"If I were still trying to please men, I would not be a servant of Christ."_ **(Galatians 1:10b)** What does all of this have to do with speaking the truth in love?

_____
_____
_____
_____
_____

3. Satan will use anybody or anything he can to get you off track an away from God. Sometimes you may feel like you are in a wrestling match. The Bible describes this conflict, _"We wrestle no against flesh and blood, but against powers and principalities..."_ **(Ephesians 6:12)** You are in a spiritual battle. List conditions and events in your life you think may confirm this.

_____

_____

_____

_____

_____

_____

4. Read **Ephesians 4:25-32.** List each of the guidelines God has given for you to follow. How will these improve your relationships?

_____

_____

_____

_____

NOTE: If you have intense and ongoing rage and bitterness at someone due to sexual abuse, support groups are available to help you work through forgiveness and healing. Talk to your group leader about finding help.

Day 5
Putting on the New Woman
Ephesians 4:17-24

1. The Bible teaches you to react in a godly manner towards others. Read the following verses, and put a check in front of the verse that most closely relates to an area in which you need to grow.

___Giving a gentle answer-**Proverbs 15:1**

___Using self-control-**Proverbs 16:32;
Proverbs 25:28; II Peter 1:5-7**
___Controlling your tongue-**Psalm 34:13;
Psalm 39:1**

2. What typically happens when you don't
follow the teaching from the verse you
chose?

_____

_____

_____

3. How can the instruction from the verse
you checked help you to love others? _____

_____

_____

_____

_____

*"But the fruit of the Spirit is love, joy, peace,
patience, kindness, goodness, faithfulness,
gentleness, and self-control."* **Galatians
5:22-23a**

4. Read **Micah 7:18-19.** Write it here in
your own words. _____

_____

_____

_____

_____

_____

_____

5. Review the names you listed in question one of this chapter. Begin to pray about each person and your relationship with him or her.

6. Collect rocks of various sizes. On the rocks write the names of people who have hurt you. The size of the rock could vary with what you think is the size of the offense. When you have finished take the rocks to a nearby pond, lake, or river. Pray the following prayer to release each one of them as you throw the rocks (offenses) into the sea of forgetfulness.

Talk to God

Dear Heavenly Father, I come before you with the fears and resentments I have been holding toward people who have offended me. It is unhealthy and wrong for me to hold onto these feelings toward _____.
I now choose, as an act of my own free will and in obedience to Your word, to release _____ to you. I trust You for the outcome. In Jesus' name I pray, Amen.

Continue until each rock has been thrown into the water as far as you can throw it.

When you repent, the Lord doesn't keep records of the wrong you've done. If He did, no one would stand a chance. **Psalm 130:3**

David writes in **Psalm 103:12**...*"as far as the East is from the West, so far has he removed our transgressions from us."*

"Remember not the sins of my youth and my rebellious ways; according to your love remember me for you are good, O Lord." **Psalm 25:7**

"May the God of peace, who through the blood of the eternal covenant brought back from the dead our Lord Jesus, the great Shepherd of the sheep, equip you with everything good for doing his will, and may he work in us what is pleasing to him, through Jesus Christ, to whom be glory forever and ever. Amen." Hebrews 13:20-21

Chapter 8

A Pool of Tears

Day 1

Depression
"An anxious heart weighs a man down..."
Proverbs 12:25a

Depression can affect you mentally, physically and spiritually. According to *Happiness is a Choice* by Paul and Jan Meier, depression in teenagers is "the psychological equivalent of the common cold because it occurs so frequently." They also write that "there's this undercurrent of feeling that depression is somehow the person's fault, and even if it's not, the person still should be able to fix it somehow; if the person stays depressed, that person has only himself/herself to blame."

Teens and young adults tend to have a harder time dealing with a crisis. You may feel like the pain won't go away and that you can't tolerate it any longer.

Symptoms
Circle the symptoms you've experienced in the past few months:

Moodiness   painful thinking
difficulty sleeping or sleeping too much
introspection (looking inward)   change in
appetite   hopelessness   anxiety

If you have symptoms that last for a long
period of time and find that they disrupt
your life, talk to your small group leader
about referring you to someone who is
qualified to help you with these issues.
Ultimately, what has helped people for
centuries that have faced loss and sorrow is
to develop a deep trust in God and his
goodness. He will not give you more that
you can handle with him, and he will walk
with you through your pain. As you come to
realize this, you will begin, at first in small
ways, to praise him for all the good gifts he
gives to you. You will be able to change
your focus from what you don't have to
what you do have.

1. What events in your life have led to
depression? _____

_____
_____
_____
_____

2. How long did it last? _____

3. Look up **Joel 2:12-14** and **Psalm 113**. Summarize the verses in a few sentences.

_____

_____

_____

_____

_____

_____

_____

_____

4. How could this teaching help you cope when you feel deep sadness?

_____

_____

_____

_____

Day 2

My Healer

God can heal you from all that affects you. **(Exodus 15:26)** The Lord records all of your tears. He knows when and why you cry. **(Psalm 56:8)**

1. Write out one of the above verses in the space provided. Circle the part that comforts you. _____

_____

_____

_____

_____

Guilt and Shame

Guilt and shame are a result of unresolved sin. If you have already confessed your sins, Satan no longer has power over you in those areas. He tends to play it back for us like a continual video clip. Stand firm on God's promise that *"if we confess our sins, he is faithful and just and will forgive us our sins and purify us from all unrighteousness."*
I John 1:9

Suicide

Suicide is sometimes brought on by a sense of hopelessness. A person may become emotionally exhausted after a major disappointment in their life and may feel that no one cares. This isn't true. God loves each person with an everlasting love.

"Praise be to the God and Father of our Lord Jesus Christ, the Father of compassion and the God of all comfort, who comforts us in all

troubles, so that we can comfort those in any trouble with the comfort we ourselves have received from God. II Corinthians 1:3-4

Read Psalm 23. In these verses David writes about feeling as though he was walking in a valley of the shadow of death. If you are obsessed with thoughts about ending your life, you need to talk to your group leader and get help. Don't let desperate feelings trick you into thinking you will always feel like this. This dark sadness will come to an end. Hold on to hope. Perhaps in this troubled time you will learn to trust God in new and life-changing ways.

You are not alone with the depth of your anguish. Read **Psalm 55:1-8, 16-19.** These verses have comforted many people when they felt there was no relief from emotional pain. Write out, in your own words, phrases from these verses that speak to you.

_____
_____
_____
_____
_____
_____
_____

Talk to God

If you feel as though your future is hopeless, talk to God about it like this.

Dear Heavenly Father, I am trying to control my life without you, and I feel so hopeless. Help me to turn over to you all areas of my life. I give control to you and choose to focus on your power to solve every problem in my life. I need to focus on you instead of on myself, and on the future rather than on the past. Be the Lord of my life in all things. In Jesus' name I pray. Amen.

Day 3
Grace, Peace, and Mercy

1. Grace is defined as unmerited favor or compassion. Look up at least three of these verses. **Hebrews 12:15; Romans 11:5-6; John 1:16-17; Ephesians 1:6-8; Romans 6:14.** What do they tell you about grace? Write what you found in your own words.

_____

_____

_____

_____

_____

_____

In what way can grace be misused? **Jude 1:4** and **Galatians 2:17-21** _____

_____

_____

_____

_____

2. Peace is a state of calm or quiet, freedom from disturbing thoughts or emotions. The Bible has a lot to say about peace. See what you discover in these verses.

Romans 5:1-2_____

Romans 14:17-18_____

John 14:27_____

Ephesians 2:14_____

Who gives us peace? _____

3. Mercy is compassion shown to an offender. Look up these verses and fill in the blanks.

Lamentations 3:22-23 *"Because of the Lord's* _____*love we are not consumed, for his* _____*never* _____. *They are* _____ *every* _____; *great is your* _____."

Psalm 25:6-7 *"Remember, O Lord, your great* _____ *and* _____,

for they are from old. Remember not the
_____ *of my* _____

and my _____ *ways."*

Day 4

1. Have you accepted God's grace, peace,
and mercy? _____ If you wrote
no, what stops you from doing so? _____

_____

Once you have accepted God's grace and
mercy and repented of your sin, Satan will
try to take you back into his control. He
doesn't want you to be right with God. He
will use family, friends, and enemies to try
to discourage you.

If this happens, remember God is in control
of everything. He is the ultimate authority.
When you face spiritual confusion and when
people oppose you, remember the following
truths:

"Do not fear, for I am with you..." **Isaiah
41:10**
"When I am afraid, I will trust in you."
Psalm 56:3
"...He is my refuge and my fortress..."
Psalm 91:2
"And so we say with confidence, The Lord is

my helper; I will not be afraid. What can man do to me? **Hebrews 13:6**

"When a man's ways are pleasing to the Lord, he makes even his enemies live at peace with him." **Proverbs 16:7**

The Full Armor of God

The way we protect ourselves from the enemy of our soul is to be filled with the Holy
Spirit and to put on the full armor of God as it tells us in **Ephesians 6:10-18:**

"Finally, be strong in the Lord and in his mighty power. Put on the full armor of God so that you can take your stand against the devil's schemes. For our struggle is not against flesh and blood, but against the rulers, against the authorities, against the powers of this dark world and against the spiritual forces of evil in the heavenly realms.

Therefore put on the full armor of God, so that when the day of evil comes, you may be able to stand your ground, and after you have done everything, to stand. Stand firm then, with the belt of truth buckled around your waist, with the breastplate of righteousness in place, and with your feet fitted with the readiness that comes from the gospel of peace.

In addition to all this, take up the shield of faith, with which you can extinguish all the flaming arrows of the evil one. Take the helmet of salvation and the sword of the Spirit, which is the word of God. And pray in the Spirit on all occasions with all kinds of prayers and requests. With this in mind, be alert and always keep on praying for all the saints."

2. What are the pieces of armor described in these verses? Underline them, then write them.

_____

_____

_____

3. What other advice did you find in these verses to protect you in spiritual battles? (Example: stand firm)

_____

_____

_____

Day 5
Read Jeremiah 31:3-4.

God promised to rebuild the nation of Israel. The book of Nehemiah is about rebuilding the wall around Jerusalem. Just as God helped this wall of protection to be rebuilt, he will help you rebuild your life. As the walls of stone were being rebuilt, the builders suffered from people working against them and mocking them. You may experience the same as you rebuild your life in Christ. Don't let this discourage you, typically the more resistance you face the more you know you are on the right track. Always remember God is faithful to protect you!

1. What does God promise the people of Israel in the verses from Jeremiah?

_____

2. Do you believe he will do the same for you?_____ Why or why not?_____

_____

_____

The story of Job is an example of a man remaining faithful to God despite his circumstances. Job went through a lot of loss and grief but refused to reject God, and in the end he was greatly rewarded.

3. Read **Job 1:13-19.** What happened to Job's family and everything he owned?

_____

_____

4. How did Job feel about this? (read verses 20-22) _____

_____

_____

In the Bible there are many other stories of people who experienced problems and almost intolerable pain. Some were brought on by their own choices or by the bad choices of others. Pain and problems are part of being human. Our goal must therefore be to learn to cope with pain and problems in a way that imitates Jesus Christ. The following verses tell about a great cloud of witnesses. These are the people living throughout history who have finished the race of life well and wait for us in heaven.

Hebrews 12:1-3 *"Therefore, since we are surrounded by such a great cloud of witnesses, let us throw off everything that hinders and the sin that so easily entangles, and let us run with perseverance the race marked out for us. Let us fix our eyes on Jesus, the author and perfecter of our faith, who for the joy set before him endured the cross, scorning its shame, and sat down at the right hand of the throne of God. Consider him who endured such opposition from sinful men, so that you will not grow weary and lose heart."*

5. According to these verses, what does sin do to you? _____

6. Who should you keep your eyes on?

_____

7. What did he endure for you?

_____

8. What was his attitude about that?

_____

9. What will happen if you think about him?

_____

_____

_____

_____

_____

Chapter 9
Looking to the Future
Day 1

Often, the last person that a post abortive woman will forgive is herself. But if you are to heal, you must reach a point where you can forgive yourself and accept the fact that you cannot change the past.

You are a completely new creation when you give your life to Christ!

1. Have you been able to accept God's forgiveness? _____
If not, try to put into words a prayer accepting the free gift of forgiveness that God offers, in order to allow you to be free from your shame and guilt. _____

_____
_____
_____
_____
_____
_____
_____

Remember, if you still struggle with feeling condemned; don't let Satan accuse you any longer. It is covered and forgotten by God through Christ's sacrifice on the cross. When Satan reminds you of what you have done, remember where he will spend eternity. Hell was created for him and the fallen angels that rebelled against God, not for you and others who have accepted Christ as their personal Lord and Savior.

2. We are more than conquerors in Christ Jesus! Read **Romans 8:35-39.** Write out verses 38-39 below.

_____
_____
_____
_____
_____

3. What are you empowered to overcome through Jesus and His love for you? _____

_____
_____
_____
_____
_____

Romans 8:9-14 teaches that once you become a follower of Jesus Christ you are no longer controlled by your sin nature. You are controlled by the Spirit of God who had the power to raise Jesus from the dead! This means that you have *supernatural* power to resist sin. These verses are not talking about willpower or resolutions; they are talking about real power to live a godly life.

4. Write a prayer admitting the power that sin has had in your life, and ask God to give you the power to stop living by your old sinful nature through the help of his Holy Spirit.

_____
_____
_____
_____
_____
_____
_____
_____
_____
_____
_____

Day 2

Letting Go of the Shame of Your Past

In order to move forward with the future God has for you, you must let go of or "renounce" the past.

1. What are some things (habits, sins, relationships, memories) from your past that you still hold on to? _____

_____

_____

Renounce means to reject or disown someone or something. **II Corinthians 4:2** talks of giving up your hidden and shameful ways. Read all of **II Corinthians 4.** If you want to have a clean heart, you must reject hidden sin (this could include involvement in the occult, New Age religions, and/or sexual sins). Then you can live in the light.

2. Write a prayer in which you give all of our past over to God's control. Be specific and really come clean before God. _____

_____

_____

_____

_____

_____

_____

_____

_____

_____

Abortion took the life of your unborn child. This child should not be looked upon as a mistake, especially if God has used this experience to bring you into an intimate, life-changing relationship with Him. We believe that you will one day meet your child in heaven, if you have accepted Christ.

3. Read **John 1:29.**

God sacrificed his only son in order to save you. He would have sacrificed his son even if you were the *only* person who needed him. He knows what it is to give up a child, he understands your grief and pain, but now he wants you to use this experience to grow and help others.

What are some ways you might be able to help others because of what you have learned?

_____

_____

_____

_____

_____

_____

"Don't copy the behavior and customs of this world, but let God transform you into a new person by changing the way you think. Then you will know what God wants you to do, and you will know how good and pleasing and perfect his will really is."
Romans 12:2 NLT

4. From the above verse, how can you know what God's will is for your life? _____

_____

_____

_____

God is Doing a New Thing!

Focus your eyes on God and what he has planned for your future. He will continue to perfect you, and you will grow in him.

"Praise be to the name of God for ever and ever; wisdom and power are his. He changes times and seasons; he sets up kings and deposes them. He gives wisdom to the wise and knowledge to the discerning. He reveals deep and hidden things; he knows what lies in darkness, and light dwells with him." **Daniel 2:20-22**

"Praise be to the God and Father of our Lord Jesus Christ, the Father of compassion and the God of all comfort, who comforts us in all our troubles, so that we can comfort those in any trouble with the comfort we ourselves have received from God."
II Corinthians 1:3-4

"For I know the plans I have for you, declares the Lord, plans to prosper you and not to harm you, plans to give you hope and

a future. Then you will call upon me and come and pray to me, and I will listen to you. You will seek me with all your heart. I will be found by you, declares the Lord..."
Jeremiah 29: 11-14a

5. From the above verse, what did you learn about God and his plans for you?

_____

_____

Talk to God

Pray this prayer for God's goals to be made known in your life.

Dear Lord of my life, I ask you to guide and direct my life. I have, through your strength, been able to forgive others and myself for my abortion. I want to move ahead with my life, but I want to follow your plan for my future, not my own. Show me through the Bible, my time in prayer with you, the church, and other Christians, what you want me to do. I also ask for strength to carry out your plan for my life. I pray this in your precious name. Amen

"Commit to the Lord whatever you do, and your plan will succeed." **Proverbs 16:3**

Day 3

God is My Strength

When you come up against spiritual struggles, remember these two verses and quote them often.

"I can do all things through him who strengthens me." **Philippians 4:13**

"...greater is he who is in you than he who is in the world." **I John 4:4 NASB**

1. Now that you are at the end of this study, what do you think God expects of you? ____

_____

_____

2. What are some ways you can use the experience of your abortion to God's glory?

_____

_____

_____

_____

Rejoice and Be Thankful

3. Read **Romans 5:10-11.** What reason to rejoice is given in these verses? _____

_____

"Rejoice in the Lord always. I will say it again: Rejoice!" **Philippians 4:4**

4. List some ways you can rejoice in the Lord. (Example: singing) _____

_____

_____

5. Think back to the beginning of this study. Name some things you are now thankful for, that you were not thankful for when you began. _____

_____

_____

_____

_____

Learn to have an attitude of gratitude, a thankful spirit, for all the good things God has given you.

"But thanks be to God, who always leads us in triumphal procession in Christ and through us spreads everywhere the fragrance of the knowledge of him."
II Corinthians 2:14

6. How does God use our thankful spirits?

_____

Day 4

Your Responsibility

If you are now a Christian who has received healing, you have some responsibilities.

"You, my brothers, were called to be free. But do not use your freedom to indulge the sinful nature; rather, serve one another in love." **Galatians 5:13**

1. Who can you serve this week? _____

_____

"Brothers, if someone is caught in a sin, you who are spiritual should restore him gently. But watch yourself, or you also may be tempted." **Galatians 6:1**

2. Write the initials of a friend who has confessed sin to you, and who you believe God wants you to help restore to a relationship with him. _____

_____

"Do not merely listen to the word, and so deceive yourselves. Do what it says."
James 1:22

3. Look back through this book. Write down three things you believe God wants you to do, based on your reading of the Word of
God._____

_____
_____
_____
_____
_____

"But the Lord said to me, ' Do not say, "I am only a child." You must go to everyone I send you to and say whatever I command you.' **Jeremiah 1:6-12 (verse 7)**

"But in your hearts set apart Christ as Lord. Always be prepared to give an answer to everyone who asks you to give a reason for the hope that you have. But do this with gentleness and respect." **I Peter 3:15**

4. Suppose a friend of yours told you that she had an abortion a few years ago and didn't understand why it was still bothering her. What reason would you give her for the hope that you have? _____

_____
_____
_____
_____
_____

Day 5

God is Faithful

Congratulations! You've stayed with the ART Bible study to the end.

1. Looking back through the book, was there ever a time when you felt like quitting?

_____

What was going on with you at that time?

_____
_____
_____
_____
_____

2. What was the most important thing you learned or did during the study? _____

_____
_____

Why? _____

_____
_____
_____

3. Look up **Philippians 1:6.** What will happen when God has begun a good work in you?

_____

4. Have you grown closer to God through this study? _____

What are some ways you can continue to grow?

_____

_____

_____

_____

_____

"Therefore, brothers, since we have confidence to enter the Most Holy Place by the blood of Jesus, by a new and living way opened for us through the curtain, that is his body, and since we have a great priest over the house of God, let us draw near to God with a sincere heart in full assurance of faith, having our hearts sprinkled to cleanse us from a guilty conscience and having our bodies washed with pure water. Let us hold unswervingly to the hope we profess, for he who promised is faithful. And let us consider how we may spur one another on toward love and good deeds. Let us not give up meeting together, as some are in the habit of doing. But let us encourage one another, and all the more as you see the day approaching." **Hebrews 10:19-25**

Appendix

Suggested Books

Woman Thou Art Loosed & Daddy Loves His Girls-
T.D. Jakes

Butterfly Kisses & Bittersweet Tears-Bob Carlisle

Growing in Christ-Nav Press

The Blessing-Gary Smalley and John Trent

I'll Hold You in Heaven-Jack Hayford

The Gift of Forgiveness-Charles Stanley

God Came Near-Max Lucado

Aborted Women, Silent No More-David Reardon

Pro-Life Answers to Pro-Choice Arguments-Randy
Alcorn

Gianna-Aborted...And Lived to Tell About It-Jessica
Shaver

Authors for Further Spiritual Growth

Kay Arthur
Joyce Meyers
Cynthia Heald
Leslie Ludy
Elisabeth Elliot
Beth Moore
Lisa Bevere
Women of Faith

Suggested Songs

Chapter One-Mind's Eye
"Mind's Eye" DC Talk-Jesus Freak
"Please Come" Nichole Nordeman-Sparrow Records

Chapter Two-Daddy's Girl
"Abba" Rebecca St. James
"Still Listening" Steven Curtis Chapman

Chapter Three- Mirror Image
"Who Are You" Barlow Girl
" I Will Be Here" Steven Curtis Chapman
Chapter Four-The Pleaser
"Never Alone" & "Surrender" Barlow Girl
"When I Fall" Rachael Lampa
"Hallowed" Jennifer Knapp
"Redeemer" Nicole C. Mullens
"I See Love" Steven Curtis Chapman

Chapter Five-Looking for Love
"Love Song" Third Day
" I Promise" Jaci Velasquez
"Without Love" Stacie Orrico

" I Am Yours" Casting Crowns

Chapter Six-Mommy
"Believe Me Now"-Steven Curtis Chapman & Mac Powell
"A Baby's Prayer" Kathy Troccoli
"Healing is in Your Hands" Christy Nockels

Chapter Seven-A Matter of Choice
"On My Knees" Jaci Velasquez
"Angels Wish" Steven Curtis Chapman

Chapter Eight-Pool of Tears
"Alabaster Box" Cece Winans
"Glory Divine" Building 429
"My Life Is In Your Hands" Kirk Franklin
"Blessings" Laura story

Chapter Nine-Looking to the Future
"Every Season" Nichole Nordeman
"I Can Only Imagine" Mercy Me
"Stay True" Stacie Orrico
"Breathe" Hungry
"Revelation Song" Kari Jobe

Praise and Worship Music

Hebrews 13:15 *"Through Jesus, therefore, let us continually offer to God a sacrifice of praise-the fruit of lips that confess his name."*

If you are troubled and unable to find a compassionate friend who understands and cares about you, listen to Christian music. Music helps us focus on who God is rather than our current circumstances. Music is powerful and it can be used for good or evil, so be careful what kind of music you listen to.

In the Bible it tells us in Psalm 95 that music was created to minister to God. II Samuel tells how David used music to calm King Saul. We can use music to praise God as well as to calm ourselves.

Vineyard Music-Hungry Series
Third Day-Offerings I & II
Star Song-Passion Series
Lakewood Church
Newsboys-Adoration
Sonic Flood
Hillsongs & Hillsongs United

Suggested Audio Tapes

"Tilly" Focus on the Family
"His Heart" Annie Graves

Suggested Video Tapes

"A Baby's Prayer" Kathy Troccoli
"Reversing Roe: The Norma McCorvey Story"

Suggested Websites

Arin, Abortion Recovery InterNational, abortionrecovery.org
David C. Reardon, elliotinstitute.org
Synda Masse, RamahInternational.org

Post Abortion Syndrome

A term first used in the early 1980s by Vincent Rue, a psychologist and trauma specialist for what he considered a form of post-traumatic stress disorder. According to the Elliot Institutes' studies woman can experience trauma from their abortion for many reasons, from the relationships that surround it and the feelings of self-betrayal, to the procedure itself. Post-Traumatic Stress Disorder (PTSD) and Post-Abortion Syndrome (PAS) symptoms are typically put in three categories; hyperarousal, intrusion, and constriction.

With **hyperarousal** the post-abortive woman develops a "fight or flight" defense mechanism. She lives in constant fear of danger. "Symptoms of hyper arousal include: exaggerated startle responses, anxiety attacks, irritability, outbursts of anger or rage, aggressive behavior, difficulty concentrating, hyper vigilance, difficulty falling asleep or staying asleep, or physiological reactions upon exposure to situations that symbolize or resemble an aspect of the traumatic experience (eg. Elevated pulse or sweat during a pelvic exam, or upon hearing a vacuum pump sound.)"

With **intrusion** the post-abortive woman re-experiences the memory of her abortion at unexpected times. "Symptoms of intrusion in PAS cases include: recurrent and intrusive thoughts about the abortion or aborted child, flashbacks in which the woman momentarily re-experiences an aspect of the abortion experience, nightmares about the abortion or child, or anniversary reactions of intense grief or depression on the due date of the aborted pregnancy or the anniversary date of the abortion."

Constriction refers to the numbing of the post-abortive woman's emotions to stimuli relating to the abortion experience. "In post-abortion trauma cases, constriction may include: an inability to recall the abortion experience or important parts of it; efforts to avoid activities or situations which may arouse recollections of the abortion; withdrawal from relationships, especially estrangement from those involved in the abortion decision; avoidance of children; efforts to avoid or deny thoughts or feelings about the abortion; restricted range of loving or tender feelings; a sense of a foreshortened future (e.g., does not expect a career, marriage, or children, or a long life.); diminished interest in previously enjoyed activities; drug or alcohol abuse; suicidal thoughts or acts; and other self-destructive tendencies."

*Quoted from David C. Reardon and The Elliot Institute, AbortionFacts.com

Post Abortion Checklist

The following symptoms are commonly experienced by people who have had an abortion.
Circle the ones that you have faced.

Anxiety
Alcohol/drug abuse
Anguish
Anger/uncontrolled outbursts
Bitterness/resentment
Change in relationships
Crying spells
Depression
Desire to be a parent
Difficulty forgiving self or others
Distancing self from others
Dizziness/fainting
Dreams/nightmares/flashbacks
Eating disorders
Emotionally numb
Emptiness
False sense of relief
Fatigue
Fear of failure
Fear of God's judgment
Fear of people finding out
Fear of pregnancy/pelvic exams
Fear of intimacy
Guilt
Headaches
Helplessness
Inferiority feelings

Infertility
Loneliness
Marital stress
Mistrust of the opposite sex
Panic attacks
Preoccupation with abortion date and/or due
date
Remorse
Sadness
Sighing
Shame
Sedative use
Sense of loss
Sexual problems
Sleeping disorders
Suicidal thoughts
Unable to relax
Weeping
Workaholic

About the Authors

Heidi Heystek

My father left my mother, my younger brother, and me for the first time when I was seven years old, for the final time when I was eight and a half. He didn't say good-bye either time. Due to this, I grew up with an intense fear of abandonment, so much so that I eventually abandoned God, myself, and my first (unborn) child at the age of sixteen on the abortion table.

After eight tormenting years, which included a miscarriage on the fifth anniversary of my abortion, I turned back to the only comfort that I had experienced growing up; my Lord and Savior, Jesus Christ with the help of a post abortion program aired by the 700 Club. I accepted God's forgiveness and was also able to forgive my father and myself. In time the Lord would even heal our father/daughter relationship.

My boyfriend and I married very young and are the parents of five grown children and one grandchild. We have helped to raise many of their friends as well. I returned to finish college and received my BA in fine arts in December of 2010 at Western Michigan University. Today my husband and I run Heystek Studios, focusing on fine art and photography. I have also become a singer/songwriter with another close friend, Jennifer Mueller.

Freedom Ministries, the post abortion outreach of Alternatives of Kalamazoo Pregnancy Care

Center, was a large part of my healing process. I would especially like to thank Robin McCastle for her godly peer counseling. You played a huge role in my recovery! I eventually became a volunteer at the Center. Freedom was dormant for a span of a few years until the Lord asked me to pick it up in 1994. Donna came shortly after and together we made an awesome team!

Along with leading multiple Bible studies, we have ministered in prison, spoken on local TV stations, and Christian and secular radio stations across the nation on post abortion healing. We've presented at Churches, Women's groups, Christian high schools and youth groups; and led trainings of various sizes. This book has become the culmination of it all. It's amazing what God can do with lives devoted to him. Someday we will look forward to meeting you as well... heidiheystek@yahoo.com

Donna Steinke

I was raised in a church going home and accepted the Lord as my personal Savior at the age of 4. At 17 I found myself in the situation of an unplanned pregnancy and had an abortion because of my own fear and the pressure of my parents to maintain their reputations in our small community. I regretted my decision even before the procedure was over and was plagued by guilt and nightmares for many years. I experienced trouble conceiving when my husband and I wanted to start a family a few years later. After many years of depression and suicidal thoughts and attempts I found healing through a Post

Abortion Support Group. After completing that group the Lord led me to Heidi and we felt led to write ART-Abortion Recovery for Teens and Twenties aimed at helping women heal at a younger age, thus sparing them from many wasted years of pain.

I was blessed by the Lord with a Godly husband, 4 children, and 4 grandchildren (and counting). I have a Bachelors Degree in Family Life Education and have spoken to groups ranging in size from 2 to over 1,500, sharing my testimony and the forgiveness offered by our Lord. I have led many post abortions support groups and was co director of Freedom Ministries, a service offered by our local pregnancy center to help women hurting from an abortion in their past. I am able to speak on the topic of abortion and to help other support group leaders learn how to work specifically with the younger women. You can contact me personally at d1steinke@aol.com